1993

To Keenan
from
Auntie
Lori & Chloe

on Your
Birthday

jungle sounds

jungle
sounds

by Rebecca Emberley

Little, Brown and Company
Boston Toronto London

First edition

Library of Congress Catalog Card Number 88-81192

10 9 8 7 6 5 4 3 2

Published simultaneously in Canada
by Little, Brown & Company (Canada) Limited

Printed in Hong Kong

for Adrian

pik a tik

snarff

snumph

snuff

hiiisssssssss

hiiisssssssss

cruncha

muncha

muncha

cruncha

SCREEOWWW

screeeeeoww

GLOSSARY OF ANIMALS AND SOUNDS

These are the sounds that the animals in this book make:

Black bird · skreee

Tiger · grrrrrrr

Rhinoceros · snarff, snumph, snuff

Pick birds eating · pik a tik

Gibbon · wook, wook, WOOK

Chimpanzee · ooh hoo hoo, aah aah, eeh eeh

Toucan · took a loo

Mandril · ook

Ants · scritch scritch

Mexican tree frog · reeeeep, reeeeep

Poison arrow frog · krroak, krroak

Fly · bzzzzzz

Frog eating · zap!

Elephant · BAARRRUUUUMMPH

Elephant walking · tromp clomp

Red bird · brreeeep

Diamondback snake · hiiisssssssssss

Giraffes eating · muncha cruncha

Parrot · awk awk

Fan-tailed lizard · nnn-gik

Gecko · nnnn-gek

Lion · ROAWR! roawr
Hippopotamuses · glub, glup, glumph
Crocodile · snap, snap
Peacock · SCREEOWWW, screeeeeoww
Butterfly · shhhhhhhhhh

Can you think of more animal sounds?

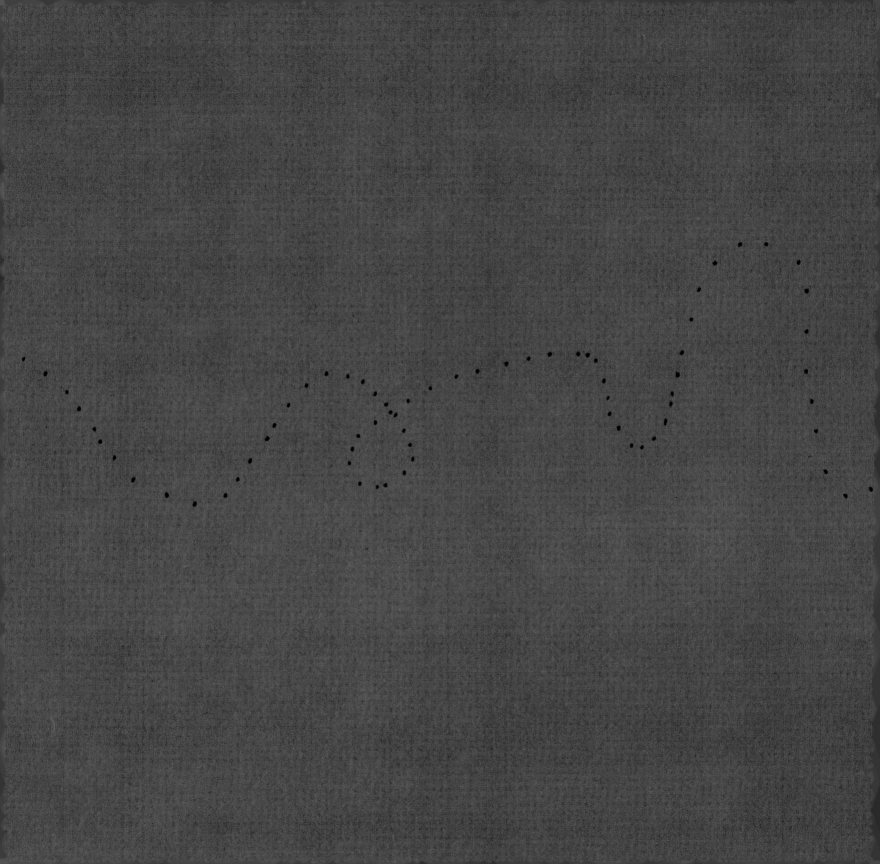

shhhhhhhhhh

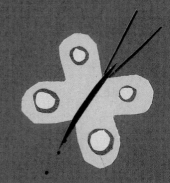